heart on my sleeve

jodi hills

TRISTAN Publishing

Minneapolis

To Quinn. This big, fashionable world awaits the revealing

of your beautiful heart.   love, aunt jodi

Library of Congress Cataloging-in-Publication Data

Hills, Jodi, 1968-
    Heart on my sleeve / written and illustrated by Jodi Hills.
        p. cm.
    ISBN 978-0-931674-87-7 (hbk. : alk. paper) 1. Women--Psychology--
Miscellanea. 2. Clothing and dress--Psychological aspects--Miscellanea.
3. Feminine beauty (Aesthetics)--Miscellanea. I.Title.

    HQ1206.H5183 2009
    155.3'33--dc22

                                                            2009009849

TRISTAN Publishing
2355 Louisiana Avenue North
Golden Valley, MN 55427

She stood in front of her hanger-filled closet and professed the words heard daily around the world,

"I have nothing to wear."

She could see the irony, as sure as the clothes that bulged from the overpacked built-in... but yet, was still paralyzed by the thought -

"I have nothing to wear."

There were jeans and
sweaters and dresses,

and memories.

"Oh, my life changed twice wearing that dress,"
she thought aloud.

She wore it the day she heard her mother had cancer,
and by chance, the same day her mother was cured.

There it was - her whole life, or at least this size of it, spread out before her. She had fallen in love in that jacket and was kissed at the coffee shop wearing those jeans. Nothing held a grudge like that orange sweater, or clung to bitter memories like that patterned scarf.

"Ok, stop it,
just pick something already..."
she tried to convince herself.

She knew it was ridiculous...
she knew it every time it happened.

And every time she promised
herself she was going to
clean out the clutter,
both in her closet and her life.

And every time she had the same arguments
with herself. "But I can't throw that, what if I get
bigger... and I can't throw that, I am going to lose
those last five pounds... and I know this will
come back in style - here just let me
try it on again... wow, when these
come back, I'm going to look
good... and remember when I..."
and the justifications
continued, while the bags
for Goodwill remained empty.

And she'd shuffle
the clothes about,
finally pick out
something, and
avoid the battle
until next week.

She had nice things. She had a lot of nice things...
The problem was, they were so entangled with
everything else. Everything else that she didn't wear
anymore, but she couldn't let go of... designer labels of
fear, worry, hurt and stagnation...

Why were these bits of material so hard to let go of...

"What should I wear?..
I have nothing...
how can I have nothing?...
I have nothing
to wear...

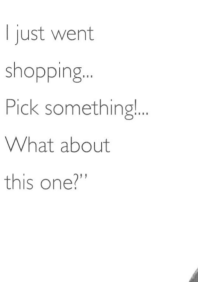

I just went
shopping...
Pick something!...
What about
this one?''

"Are you kidding me, he's already seen me in that... What about this? - Oh, she'd laugh at me then... Or this? - never again... but maybe, just not today....

Pick something!"

"I   have   nothing   to   wear..."

As she internally screamed it to the heavens,

someone or something must have heard her,

because at that very moment, the entire rod let go from the wall and all of her "nothing to wear" came crashing to the floor.

She took a deep breath and

said to the fashion powers that be -

"I'll think of something..."

Maybe it was a sign, or a loose screw -

both literally and figuratively -

either way, she knew things had to change.

It was time to let a few things go.

If it didn't fit her life in that moment, she
had to let it go. If she didn't look good
in it anymore, she had to let it go.

She had let go of the
man she fell in love with
in that jacket,

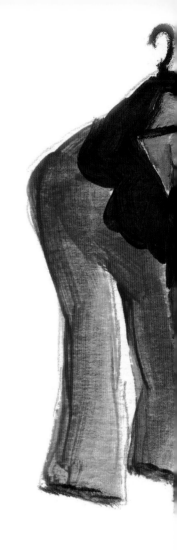

perhaps it was time to let

the jacket go as well.

She changed jobs in that
suit, and dreams in that
dress, yet the past just
hung there.

Times change, people
change, and lives change
- just as sure as trends
and styles.

She had grown so much through the years, and she looked good - she glowed from within.

She didn't need to have this constant struggle...
she knew what she needed to wear now, and she looked good in it.

She wore her
wardrobe of hope
and happiness and
confidence well...
it fit her close in all
the right places and
was always,
and exactly
her color.

She didn't need her closet, or her thoughts,
cluttered with fear and bitterness and loss,
packed with "what was" and "what could be",
but the beauty of happily right now.

Her heart would fit her wardrobe and was much more reliable than "one size fits most." She knew there would be some danger wearing it so close to the surface... but it went with everything she had, and it made her feel beautiful...

After cleaning,
and still believing
"you are what you
wear," she placed her
heart on her sleeve
and knew she would
be fabulous!